WINDOW DECORATING

SECOND EDITION

The Hunter Douglas Guide to

WINDOW
DECORATING

SECOND EDITION

The Complete Reference for Designing
Beautiful Window Treatments

Creative Direction by Miriam Feinseth

Text by Jill Kirchner and Carol Sama Sheehan

Design by Paul Hardy

Window treatments have evolved into an art form that superbly blends the practical with the aesthetically pleasing. On the cover, Silhouette window shadings preserve the view while softening the light flooding through a summer home's wrap-around porch windows. The same shadings create an understated backdrop for bold sculpture in a contemporary setting, previous page. Luminette Privacy Sheers, left, have a barely-there simplicity that enhances the architectural grace of French doors. Following page, thanks to the PowerRise battery-operated remote-control system, pale pink Duette honeycomb shades in a neutral window-lined study can be raised or lowered at the touch of a button. Pages 8 and 9, Country Woods blinds meld the classic beauty of wood with the crisp clarity of white in a modern bay window.

Published by American HomeStyle and Gardening/Gruner+Jahr USA Publishing, 375 Lexington Avenue, New York, New York 10017

Manufactured in China

ISBN 0-9636751-3-3

Second Edition

FOREWORD

The world of window fashions, more than any other area of home design, has undergone dramatic change and diversification in recent years. Technological advances and refinements in style have elevated the treatment of windows to an art, and Hunter Douglas has led the way.

The purpose of this book is to guide you through the many fashionable window covering options available today. It will also explain how these options can meet your needs for privacy, security, light control, and energy efficiency as well as ease of maintenance and operation. The ultimate goal? For you to create the most aesthetically pleasing and practical window fashions for your interiors.

Fashion, function, and quality are hallmarks of Hunter Douglas, the premier manufacturer of custom window coverings. Known as *the* innovator in the field, Hunter Douglas has consistently won universal acclaim for the flawless combination of high tech and high style of its products.

Today, the diverse Hunter Douglas product line includes Luminette Privacy Sheers and SIlhouette window shadings—soft, sheer looks that also provide privacy and light control—as well as versatile and energy-efficient Duette honeycomb shades and Vignette window shadings, a dramatically improved version of the classic Roman shade. The most up-to-date options in aluminum blinds, wood blinds, vertical blinds, pleated and window shades, shutters, cornices, valances, and moldings are available as well. In addition, Hunter Douglas offers remote control motorization that is as simple as it is affordable and a multitude of hardware systems to suit virtually any window.

To make the window an integral element of interior design, we also offer fabric by the yard, draperies, top treatments, bed coverings, and decorative accessories that complement all Hunter Douglas window covering products—in short, everything for the well-dressed window.

We hope the information and photography in this book will help you select the ideal window fashions for your home and bring unlimited satisfaction to you, your family, and your friends.

Some thanks are in order, especially to the editors of *American HomeStyle and Gardening*, a Gruner + Jahr publication, for working with us to create such a beautiful and informative book.

If we can be of further assistance in your quest to find window treatment solutions, please call us at 1-800-937-STYLE, or contact us via e-mail at consumer@hunterdouglas.com. Or visit the Hunter Douglas website: www.hunterdouglas.com.

Marvin Hopkins

MARVIN HOPKINS
PRESIDENT AND CEO, HUNTER DOUGLAS INC.

STYLE
AND DECORATION

Successful window treatments introduce a combination of style and decoration to a room that is appropriate both for the visual setting and for the role of the room. While "style" usually refers to the overall look of a design scheme and "decoration" to its flourishes and details, these two elements are inseparable in the art of creating beautiful and enduring window fashions.

Window fashions have come a long way since animal skins and oilcloth were thrown across the tiny apertures that passed for windows in primitive dwellings. The word "window," from the Norse, literally means "eye of the house through which the wind enters." As early as the 17th century, glazed windows with small panes of glass began to grace homes in Europe and the New World, along with simple wood shutters and plain cloth curtains. Yet not until the advent of mass-produced glass in the 19th century did glazed windows become a universal luxury.

Since that time, all shapes, styles, and sizes of windows have emerged, and, along with them, an astounding variety of techniques and materials for enhancing windows. In recent years, the simultaneous rise of new technologies and emergence of a cogent design philosophy for treating windows has made the art of window fashions just that—an art that can bring beauty and comfort to every room in your house.

Elaborate window decor with ornate draperies and top treatments is characteristic of the Louis XVI period.

As with any domestic art, window fashions should serve both practical and aesthetic purposes.

The style in which you treat your windows will be determined in part by pragmatic considerations. The window type; the need to control light, heat, or cold entering from the outside; the desire for security, quiet, comfort, and privacy—all these factors will affect the decisions you make about window treatments.

Important aesthetic factors will also influence the way you choose to dress your windows. The architectural style of the house often points the way to the most handsome and appropriate window treatments. To be faithful to an old-fashioned Victorian house, for example, you might choose billowing curtains with swags, fringe, and lace panels. Or you might tone down the period display with a combination of wood blinds and loosely swagged top treatment. In a standard-issue city apartment, a luxurious balloon fabric shade over a translucent window shading system can establish a distinctive decor for the entire room. In a country home, wood shutters and ruffled valances might be most seemly for the heart of the home, the living room or keeping room.

The design of the room setting, including its furniture, must be carefully considered when planning new window treatments. With so many decorating choices today—from English country to Shaker, Arts and Crafts style to Bauhaus, postmodern to western—the world of window fashions has expanded to make it possible to coordinate any style you fancy.

In a sleek, contemporary room where light and space are the dominant elements, horizontal miniblinds hung floor to ceiling over the window area make a dramatic statement without be-

Previous pages, in a seaside setting, Luminette Privacy Sheers in softly textured Linea fabric allow sunlight to gently flow through a window-lined wall while softening glare. The adjustable vanes can be rotated closed to control privacy and light.

ing obtrusive. Palladian windows can be outfitted with cellular light-filtering shades customized to fit within each arch. For bay windows, another style that places a unique stamp on a room, vertical blinds are available that fit closely into the bend of the window and help you to make the most of the bay as well as project the right look. The use of any of a host of specialty fabrics for blinds and shades makes myriad room schemes possible. And the tailored look of fabric-like shades complements virtually any style or decor.

The principal function of the room will also suggest the most logical solutions for its windows. Curtains, draperies, top treatments, and fabric shades add romance and intimacy in a bedroom. The home office, increasingly common, comes into its own as a comfortable sanctuary for work, with softer window treatments using fabric in subtle patterns and colors instead of the purely utilitarian and often sterile commercial office arrangements.

Given the sophistication and diversity of window fashions, you might think deciding how to treat your own windows will be difficult. The fact is, window fashions are responsive to the precise personal tastes in furnishings, fabrics, art, and collectibles that inform every room with style. There are "hard" window treatments, "soft" window treatments, and combinations of the two, offering beautiful solutions for windows of every kind.

Hard window treatments include shutters, shades, and

Beyond Woods hardwood blinds bring new sophistication to wood blinds with elegant finishes such as burled walnut, shown here, and bird's-eye maple.

blinds made of metal, vinyl, or wood. Hard treatments are often more utilitarian than soft ones, though they may also be decorative; they are appreciated for their simple, streamlined look and their capacity to control light.

Soft window treatments encompass draperies, curtains, window shadings, soft shades, and top treatments and trimmings. (Although the terms "curtains" and "draperies" are sometimes used interchangeably, curtains are generally considered to be soft window coverings gathered onto a wood or metal rod, while draperies are pleated fabric coverings suspended by hooks from traverse rods or other carriers.) Soft treatments use fabric to enrich windows and rooms with color, pattern, and texture. Unlike hard treatments, they can carry out a room's decorative theme or pattern, add a generous note of opulence, and even stand on their own as focal points of interior design.

Hard/soft window treatments combine elements of both types. Borrowing the best of both worlds often provides the ideal solution for window treatments. When the practical merits of blinds and shades are combined with the aesthetic benefits of fabrics, windows become much more than "the eye of the house through which the wind enters."

A large bow window is dressed in formal draperies with swagged valances and shirred Austrian sheers, connoting elegance in a traditionally furnished living room.

Sheer panels of patterned lace soften the lines of tall louvered shutters in a Victorian bedroom, left. The wooden shutters create privacy, while the romantic lace, hung on simple brass rings and rods, filters the afternoon light. Lace sheers were a traditional undertreatment for Victorian draperies, but used alone they have an airy, unencumbered feeling. Above right, a single silk taffeta curtain, shirred on a rod with Roman shade undertreatment, provides dramatic window dressing for a highly stylized reading nook. A room filled with images of antiquity, below right, is graced by a drapery edged with Greek key trim and tied back for elegant effect. The Roman shade diffuses the light and also ensures privacy.

The cascading folds of Vignette window shadings in a crisp seersucker, left, provide softly diffused light as well as complete privacy in a bath. Vignette window shadings have the tailored appearance of Roman shades (seen at right in a country dining room), but can be easily raised and lowered without wrinkling or sagging. When raised, the shadings are completely concealed within the headrail. The fabric folds are attached to a soft knit panel that provides a uniform appearance from the street side. Traditional Roman shades sewn from fabric, right, gather into flat, broad pleats for a trim appearance neatly contained within the window frame.

Great views are the delight of any city dweller, but privacy is an equally compelling need. Duette Manhattan shades in a refined linen texture enhance the strong architectural lines of this loft, and their versatile top-down/bottom-up configuration lets them welcome light through the top of the window while screening visibility below, or vice versa.

Properly selected, window treatments contribute just the right combination of function and fashion to a room. Perforated vertical blinds, left, suit the cutting-edge attitude of a sleek Eurostyle kitchen, outfitted with granite counters and stainless steel appliances. Luminette Privacy Sheers, right, take the concept one step further. Adjustable vanes are attached to a sheer knit fabric facing, providing the best features of both sheers and blinds. In this gracious parlor, Luminette sheers hang beneath elegantly swagged curtains just as traditional sheers would, but offer the additional benefit of being able to control light and privacy.

Classic Palm Beach shutters unadorned by draperies make a bold linear statement at a sunny window. Made of PolySatin vinyl, these Hunter Douglas shutters do more than control light; unlike wood, they actually resist fading and cracking even after prolonged exposure to strong sunlight. Right, opaque Duette shades darken a cozy, richly toned southwestern bedroom. These shades have a metallic blackout core that helps keep the strong desert sun at bay. When full sunlight is desired, the shades stack compactly, leaving the entire window in the clear.

In a converted barn with few sources of illumination, Duette honeycomb shades permit filtered light to infuse the space with warmth. The shades offer an unobtrusive counterpoint to the rustic furnishings.

pulent Austrian shades with their soft gathers and scalloped edges imbue a spacious country bathroom with romance, left. The fabric draws up into elegant folds, or ruches, across its entire width. Austrian shades can be made in fabrics ranging from simple ticking to delicate silks. Here, a colorful chintz echoes views of the garden outside. Curtains have a more neutral presence in a creamy monochromatic bedroom, right, but the lush fullness of fabric adds softness and warmth to the room nonetheless. These simply gathered curtains have been hung on distinctive wrought iron rods mounted close to the ceiling to enhance the impression of height.

In a room featuring classical architecture but an open, modern approach to space, Silhouette window shadings create a subtle backdrop with timeless appeal. The sheer fabric mutes the intensity of the sun streaming through full-length windows while still offering a soft-focus view of the greenery outdoors. By tilting or closing the adjustable fabric vanes, greater privacy or light control can be achieved. Silhouette is an ideal way to protect high-quality textiles such as this rug, wood floors, and other fine furnishings from the damaging effects of the sun.

For this grandly scaled bedroom, an expansive arched window is cut down to size by the addition of a floral swag. Below it, two-inch aluminum blinds by Hunter Douglas neatly dress a pair of windows; above the swag, the half-round window is left unadorned to serve as a constant source of natural light.

A converted barn's oversize, unusually tall windows call for the simple solution of Country Woods two-inch wood blinds. The color stain complements the old oak flooring while the horizontal slat pattern adds a linear dimension to a wall of vintage barnboard.

et in as much or as little of the world as you like: Vignette window shadings let you frame the view, shade the sun, or warm up a cold, dark expanse of glass at night. The clean, tailored lines of these fabric shades suit this casual, contemporary sunroom as well as more formal settings. Vignette window shadings marry the inherent warmth and soft luminescence of fabric with the controlled ease of operating a shade—and they disappear completely inside a sleek headrail when you just want to sit back and enjoy the view.

THE RIGHT LIGHT

Natural light is the soul of a room, a tangible presence in house or workplace that allows the occupants to experience the changing seasons and times of day. The amount of light that is appropriate or desirable varies from room to room. Window treatments help us to bask in the light, to artfully screen and filter it, and, when need be, to restrict it completely.

Traditional venetian blinds, such as these Country Woods blinds by Hunter Douglas, provide a simple yet effective way to control light and views.

Film directors and impressionist painters have at least one thing in common with successful window fashion designers—an understanding of light.

What moviegoer hasn't been affected by the dramatic lighting of a scene—afternoon sunlight streaming melodramatically through venetian blinds into the private eye's office, or a pair of lovers walking along a beach, romantically backlit by the setting sun? What museumgoer hasn't been transfixed before one of Monet's giant canvases, shimmering with enough light to nurture a thousand flower gardens?

The subtle yet powerful effect of light on human beings is just as noticeable in the private home. Windows and window fashions provide the means for us to use natural light in the most beneficial ways, enjoying it to the fullest, yet able to control it.

Make no mistake about it, light, especially natural light, makes us feel better, physically and emotionally. Usually without realizing it, we enjoy the changing conditions of light as each day

Previous pages, silky Silhouette window shadings provide an understated yet rich undertreatment for a lush drapery. The detail reveals the innovative architecture of Silhouette, with adjustable fabric vanes suspended between sheer knit layers.

and each season unfolds. For our sense of well-being and happiness, it is in our interest to bring as much natural light into our homes as possible. Window fashions help to light rooms in a way that is both practical and pleasing to the eye.

"Practical" cannot be overlooked, for a window full of light by day may resemble a black void by night, robbing the dwellers of privacy and making them uneasy. Blinds, shutters, shades, and layered fabric treatments restore a sense of security and intimacy without compromising the luxury of light by day.

The orientation of your windows, their size, shape, and placement, and the window treatments you select together determine how effectively natural light illuminates your interiors.

The direction your windows face—their exposure—is your first consideration. North-facing windows bring in the clearest, most even and consistent light, which is why this exposure is preferred for artists' studios. This light has a cool, bluish cast. In northern climates, builders limit the number of windows on the north side because it is the coldest exposure. For energy conservation, those windows are often treated with insulated fabric shades, shutters, lined draperies, and cornices.

East-facing windows admit warmer, brighter light, especially in the morning. For this reason, they are often treated with materials that diffuse light, such as pleated shades, window shadings, sheers, woven blinds, and shutters.

Windows that face west are exposed to the hottest light—and also the haziest, due to the fact that by day's end, there are so many more impurities in the atmosphere. Because prolonged exposure to this strong light can be damaging to wood furniture and colored fabrics, especially in summer, west windows are generally covered with any one or a combination of light-diffusing

treatments, including vertical or horizontal blinds, honeycomb or pleated shades, shutters, and sheers.

South-facing windows, the most important natural-light source in any building because they receive sunlight year-round, cast a warm, golden glow on interiors. Again, some combination of light-diffusing window treatments helps protect fabric and furniture in rooms on that side of the house.

The manner in which natural light comes into a room is also affected by window location. Windows high on an exterior wall admit light deep into the room, while low or wide windows bring in the light in shallow swaths. In small rooms, the presence of several windows will offer a more even distribution of natural light; so will groupings of windows in a large space.

Light also falls into a room in colors and patterns that are affected by the exterior atmosphere and landscape and by window treatments themselves. Shimmering puddles of summer light, filtered through a tree's foliage onto a floor, add a romantic dimension to a living room. Equally dramatic effects are felt when sunlight pours through

The opaque Duette shade, here in a bottom-stacking configuration, provides light-filtering shade by day, right, and blackout-dense privacy by night, left.

lace curtains, shutter louvers, window shadings, or the slats of blinds.

Materials selected for window treatments can harness natural light to pleasing effect. When sunlight streams through diaphanous fabrics or translucent pleated shades of white, rose, or yellow, the room is cast in similar hues. For a window with an unsightly view, a cellular shade combining translucent and opaque fabrics draws in light by day and protects privacy at night. In bathrooms, opaque coverings such as wood blinds, miniblinds, shades with privacy backings, or window shadings provide elegant solutions. In an east-facing bedroom, room-darkening shades, accompanied by curtains, can block out dawn's early light but be opened to welcome afternoon sun.

A new generation of skylights and greenhouse windows offers dramatic ways to incorporate natural light into home design. Master bedroom spas, sun porches, atria, and conservatories all have gained charm and livability from the advanced technologies in treatments for such windows. Miniblinds, vertical blinds, and fabric shades with built-in insulation provide stylish systems for controlling light, ventilation, and exposure to cold air in winter climates, or for basking in full sun in the interior space.

Silhouette window shadings can be tilted closed, as the shade is on the left, for privacy and gentle light, or rotated open, as on the right, to permit more light and clearer visibility.

French doors in a cottage bedroom, left, are fitted with versatile Luminette Privacy Sheers, which combine the softness of sheer curtains with the adjustability of blinds. The sheers can be opened to welcome in the outdoors during the day or closed for diffused light, and the vertical vanes can be tilted partially or completely closed for greater privacy. Their unobtrusive presence doesn't upstage the quirky charms of this picture-lined summer haven. Gently waved Vignette window shadings, right, come in a range of tones and textures such as this linen weave that transforms harsh or gray light into a golden glow. Unlike conventional fabric shades, the contoured folds hold their shape indefinitely, resisting wrinkling and drooping.

As the dramatic focal point in a formal setting, a towering wall of glass brings architectural interest and abundant natural light into a room. Elegantly simple sheer fabric Silhouette window shadings, installed on the glass doors, uniquely combine the functions of shade and blind. They permit an unobstructed view when open, yet safeguard privacy when closed.

Light is controlled at a tall window in a modern room, left, with sleek horizontal aluminum miniblinds that seamlessly integrate a curved headrail and valance with the spring-tempered slats. Right, in a more rustic country setting, Nantucket window shadings, an informal version of Silhouette window shadings, softly set the scene for timeworn furnishings graced with the patina of age. Window shadings are the newest, most versatile way to gently filter light or wrap a room in a velvety cocoon of shade.

Pleated shades from Hunter Douglas ensure privacy for a bedroom, left, without depriving the occupant of light streaming through the leaded glass panes. A Carole Fabrics chintz overtreatment adds a welcome splash of color. In an old-fashioned kitchen where sunlight is important and the view is not, right, vertical blinds act as a privacy screen without intruding on the charm of the room.

The versatility of Luminette Privacy Sheers, explained at a glance: When drawn open, top, the sheers gather into soft folds like a traditional drapery. When drawn across the window, the vanes can be rotated open to invite in the view, right, or closed with the simple twist of a wand, above, for privacy typically unavailable in a sheer.

In a streamlined modern office, left, vinyl vertical blinds diffuse the glare of sunlight (particularly problematic when working with computers) and create a quiet backdrop that won't distract from the business of work. At home, top right, bright white Duette PowerRise honeycomb shades behind a decorative fabric top treatment fill a kitchen with soft filtered light. An assortment of small, fixed windows in the corner apartment of a high-rise, bottom right, required a uniform but understated treatment. Two-inch Country Woods blinds with a sandblasted finish blend with the walls when closed, and take advantage of sunny days when opened.

PATTERN TEXTURE AND COLOR

The height of window decoration occurs when the richness of fabric and other materials is introduced. Not all windows call for opulent treatment, but when it is appropriate, the window can become a compelling statement. The orchestration of color, pattern, and texture, echoing the room decor and tempered by natural light, brings the window to its fullest realization as an expression of design.

The amount of decoration appropriate to a window depends on the role it serves in the room setting. That may be a subordinate, supporting, or starring role.

The window plays a subordinate role in the overall decor, for example, when its view is so desirable—a cityscape by night, a garden, a bit of countryside—that to treat the window elaborately would distract from the vista. Such a window should be dressed so simply, with neutral lines and wall-matching color, that the treatment recedes into the background. In a subordinate role, the window says, in effect, "Look through me."

In a supporting role, by contrast, it says, "Look at the room." When playing this role, the window receives a higher degree of decoration in order to link it to the architectural style or interior design. More fabric is incorporated to coordinate with the room's furnishings.

Soft yet crisply tailored, pleated shades can be used alone or as an undertreatment for draperies.

In a starring role, the window declares, "Look at me!" Generally, windows are called upon to serve as focal points in rooms otherwise devoid of a visual center of attention. A room with a handsome fireplace or wonderful works of art probably doesn't need to have its windows singled out for lavish treatment. But a room lacking distinctiveness can be transformed by dramatic window fashions.

No matter what role a window is given, the judicious use of color, pattern, and texture is crucial to the success of its treatment. These are the three building blocks of window style.

Previous pages, honey-toned Vignette window shadings in a rich linen weave diffuse a golden glow whatever the weather. Its soft, easy-gliding folds (detail) make Vignette superior to traditional Roman shades. Right, the deep jewel tone of Duette shades offers an instant route to drama in a study.

Treating a window is not unlike coordinating a wardrobe, demanding the same concern for comfort, good taste, and fashion. Just as we dress differently for different occasions, windows call for a variety of styles. Some windows are meant to remain discreetly in the background and are dressed in a neutral style, comparable to conservative business attire. Others are the visual centerpiece of the room and deserve the same attention as the wardrobe mistress gives her diva on opening night.

A formal house and lifestyle will entail window fashions of greater sophistication and complexity than an informal abode. In choosing fabrics, formality is evoked with shimmering silks and taffetas, informality with soft cottons and polished chintzes.

Shutters add character and coziness to a room enjoyed as a library or family room. Wood shutters may be stained or painted to coordinate with any wall color. PVC shutters offer much the same character and are appropriate for more casual areas.

Horizontal and vertical blinds come in a wide spectrum of colors and textures. Miniblinds in metallic finishes are right at home in a high-tech interior. Wood blinds and wrapped wood blinds, in a range of natural finishes, colors, and textures, combine effectively with curtains and top treatments. Vertical blinds impose a handsome, drapery-like pattern on a window and, with fabric vanes, become draperies themselves, coordinating with a room's other fabric patterns.

Pleated shades, a relative newcomer, are among the most versatile window coverings available. They come in hundreds of colors and fabrics, letting you bring the look of lace, linen, silk, or even satin to your windows. Cellular shades provide a seamless honeycomb design in textures such as linen, raw silk, or tweed, or with marble, granite, or other faux finishes. Another innovation, window shadings, combines the softness of a fabric shade with the function of blinds in a range of light-filtering colors. Privacy sheers, even more translucent, also incorporate adjustable vanes for light control.

Soft window fashions offer the most opportunity for asserting personal style. Unlike hard treatments, which usually are limited to the dimensions of the window frame, soft treatments can be used to surround the window and create a dramatic focus.

Fabric shades bring the visual and tactile properties of textiles to windows and can be used in a multitude of settings. With their voluminous pleats and poufs, Austrian and balloon shades have a sumptuous, opera-house elegance. Crisp, tailored Roman shades can be as decorative as the pattern of the fabric from which they're made. Most important, they are a means of introducing bold or subtle touches of color, texture, and pattern.

Top treatments and trimmings are decorator touches used to customize window fashions. Valances and cor-

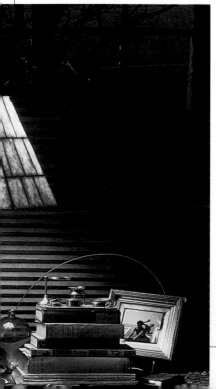

A large-scale floral matched with a stripe and a subdued damask, all from Carole Fabrics, creates a feminine look.

nices incorporate many materials—wood, ironwork, fabric—and can be trimmed with such flourishes as welting, braid, and fringe. Fabric valances can be shirred and shaped, pleated and tabbed. Wood cornices in varying profiles (wide or narrow, simple or ornate) add architectural detail; they may be upholstered, painted, or antiqued.

Monochromatic color schemes using neutral colors are the simplest to devise. A creamy white pleated shade with a lacy texture might be paired with beige curtains in a room with beige walls. In a more formal setting, a monochromatic scheme might be used to visually outline and embellish a window with curtains, passementerie, and fringe, with matching undershade.

A coordinated color scheme might link a window treatment with an upholstery fabric. A paisley valance could complement the paisley on a sofa, for instance, set off by wood blinds in the print's background color. In a contrasting scheme, English country chintz curtains and a sheer balloon shade might be paired with a striped slipper chair. Or, in a richly paneled room, a window hung in deep-toned draperies might be crowned with an asymmetrical swag and jabot in a complementary hue.

Whether in a cozy family room, dignified library, or utilitarian home office, wood blinds add warmth and tailored sophistication. These blinds from the Country Woods collection lend a honeyed radiance to this neutral but richly textured scheme. Wood-tone finishes, ranging from bleached pine to deep mahogany, offer a subtle complement to almost any color palette. When greater light control is desired, the exclusive de-Light feature from Hunter Douglas eliminates the light leakage through cord holes that is typical of horizontal blinds.

Don't overlook the potential of color to add distinctive style when selecting a window treatment. Pleated shades in green, left, harmonize with the deep hunter-green walls of this living room, establishing a monochromatic background for the pattern of the sumptuous Austrian shade and the room's tailored furnishings. A lighter, retro spirit is evoked by the combination of a 1940s-inspired curtain fabric, right, and wide-slatted Country Woods blinds that fit the period feel. Green wood slats are sparked with the unexpected accent of sunny yellow tape—just two of the myriad color choices available in wood finishes and tape trim.

Neutral window fashions can blend in, contrast with a room's decor, or even dominate a subtle color scheme. Cool white pleated shades accent the textured beige walls in a casual room, left. The emphasis is reversed in a bathroom, below left, where privacy-guarding gray roller shades make a dramatic statement against the creamy walls. In a pale, warm hue that blends into the understated scheme at right, versatile pleated shades offer top-down/ bottom-up operation and are fitted to the quarter- and half-round windows as well.

oday's aluminum blinds in all their variety make an important contribution to the coordinated look of a room. Pale pink microblinds with half-inch slats, left, blend pleasingly with the wall color. Right, broad two-inch white blinds are animated with crisp blue tapes to match the graphic lines and colorful energy of a crayon-bright dining room.

The Beyond Woods collection brings decorative richness to hardwood blinds by wrapping solid wood slats with distinctive veneers such as bird's-eye maple or burled mahogany. In a country bedroom, right, whitewashed blinds echo the light, informal feel of the pale pine woodwork. In an eat-in kitchen, left, standard windows get a custom look from blinds with a stippled-paint surface.

White or neutral shades work beautifully with almost any color and decor. Here, Silhouette window shadings enhance the richness of the room's muted golds and greens without competing with them. The broad three-inch vanes recall the graphic style of plantation shutters and open up a wider view of the outdoors. The clean-lined look of Silhouette is carried through to the coordinating headrail, which completely conceals the shade when it's raised, and the single control cord—no messy multiple support cords to interrupt the view.

64

Hunter Douglas pleated shades in a rich jewel tone from the Kashmir collection, right, update a chic 1920s European color palette. Top-down operation provides privacy plus natural light. In a monochromatic, rosy-beige attic room with a series of angled skylights, top left, neutral-colored vinyl verticals were chosen so that the direction and intensity of sunlight streaming in could be easily modulated. The Hunter Douglas Vertical Specialty System makes verticals ideally suited to skylights as well as to curved, angled, bay, and bow windows. Always take into consideration what your window treatments will look like from the outside: Luminette Privacy Sheers, bottom left, like many Hunter Douglas products, have vanes with neutral coloring on the outer surface to ensure a clean, uniform appearance from the exterior, no matter what the coloration inside. When the vanes are open, the soft facing fabric transmits a golden glow while obscuring interior details.

WINDOWS BY
DESIGN

Just as a picture frame sets off a painting, a window enhances the view from within and without. The window's shape and style, and its purpose—to take advantage of great scenery, simply to admit light, to add architectural interest—help to determine the best treatment. The fine art of window decorating lies in serving good design where it is found, and in providing good design where it is lacking.

In the Middle Ages, the glazier's art produced windows of such beauty that when noble families moved from one castle to the next, they took their windows along. Thanks to today's sophisticated window fashions, modern homeowners appreciate their windows almost as much, and with good reason. Properly treated, window fashions play an important role in successful interior design, helping rooms to come alive with light, color, and character.

In designing window treatments—light control and privacy being the primary concerns—it is helpful to evaluate each window in four ways: 1) as an individual unit, 2) in relation to other windows, 3) in relation to the room's style and design, and 4) as seen from the outside looking in.

A window may first be identified by type; that alone often suggests the direction your treatment should take. For instance, French doors that swing open and patio doors that slide open require shades or blinds with different operating systems. Standard sash and picture windows lend themselves

An arch window adds charm and historic flavor to a house's architecture.

to a multitude of hard and soft solutions. The unique architectural details of arch and bay windows are greatly enhanced by the correct window treatment. Clerestory windows high on a cathedral ceiling or round portholes demand specialized treatments. There are equally effective custom solutions for skylights, unusually shaped windows, and glass walls.

If the size or shape of a window is unsatisfactory, a fabric treatment can be devised to make it appear larger or smaller, taller or wider than it really is. In this way, the art of window fashions compensates for deficiencies of style and function often found in older houses or those that have undergone awkward remodeling.

Just as a beautiful frame enhances a painting, window frames with distinctive structural features, such as pilasters, pediments, fanlights, or arches, add drama to the window. A window with a visually interesting surround would be treated differently—perhaps only with unobtrusive blinds or shades—than one with no notable architectural outline.

Evaluating the window's context yields other clues to the most appropriate way to treat it. In traditional houses, such as Cape Cods or Colonials, window placement is usually orderly and balanced, while in newer buildings, a random, even whimsical pattern is often the rule.

A window by itself on a wall can be treated independently. But windows are often hung in pairs or larger groupings, and a suitable treatment must encompass the set. If two windows different in height are paired on a wall, they can be transformed into

Previous pages, a casement window trimmed in a lively color is well served by Duette honeycomb shades that allow enjoyment of the view when raised. Left, Duette lends itself to an elegant fan-like treatment for a half-round.

twins simply by mounting drapes, valances, or cornices at a matching height above each window frame, so the shorter appears to be the same size as the taller. Similarly, adjacent windows can be disguised as one by hanging draperies to conceal the wall space between.

The most important step in designing window treatments is evaluating the window in relation to the style of the room. Formal rooms usually call for attention to detail at the window. Rich fabrics and elegant ornamentation help to bring such a room together in a harmonious scheme. Informal rooms, however, may require simpler solutions. When furnishings are casual and unpretentious, unduly sumptuous windows run the risk of fussiness and overstatement.

Rooms with a period stamp generally benefit from window treatments that acknowledge the style. Ornate top treatments, such as pelmets or cornices with panels of rich brocade, would look out of place in a simple Colonial room but are authentic additions to one in Elizabethan or Baroque style. When pelmets, cornices, or valances are used, an effective top treatment may imitate a dominant shape in the room, such as the outline of a fireplace mantel or sofa back. Similarly, fabric patterns

A new home in traditional shingle style uses modern window design to invite in light. Window coverings have evolved to suit options from French doors to Palladian windows to skylights.

Duette honeycomb shades, here with Skyrise hardware, can be adapted to fit skylights and windows on angled walls.

used at the window can agreeably echo those found in a room's furnishings, promoting a cohesive design.

Historic accuracy isn't always desirable. In a true Victorian parlor, windows were covered with heavy draperies and large swags, but this decor produces a room most of us today would find dark and depressing. Today's Victorian-house dweller sensibly cuts back on period trappings, opting perhaps for lacy shades in ornately carved surrounds.

Finally, it's wise to visualize how treatments will appear from outside the house. Aesthetically, window fashions should go virtually unnoticed from the outside, yet contribute to the architectural character of the house. No single window should stand out, nor should drapery, blind, or shade colors clash with the facade. Windows adjacent to each other but treated in markedly different styles also distract from the house's appearance as a unified entity.

You needn't resort to an uninteresting uniformity in window treatments to achieve a design that's successful from inside and out. But the Mies van der Rohe dictum "Less is more" is worth heeding. Variations can be introduced from room to room with considerable flair that accomplish your decorating goals without destroying the harmony of the exterior.

A large fixed-glass window positioned to make the most of this beach house's ocean views is covered with a sheer Duette shade by Hunter Douglas, which offers optimal transparency. The knit fabric shade has been installed to permit raising from the bottom or lowering from the top. The same product, with its honeycomb construction, is versatile enough to cover specialty window shapes such as the room's porthole window as well.

Graceful arch windows, left, a focal point in almost any room, are often left uncovered if there is no need for privacy or light control. In this playroom, Duette honeycomb shades meet practical needs without detracting from architectural beauty. The arch shades and the rectangular window shades are separate installations. A Duette honeycomb shade in a buttery hue works equally well in a more feminine setting, right, where a window set into its own niche is framed by draperies that accent the roof's gable.

The wide range of looks that can be achieved with window treatments, and the way they set the style for an entire room, is illustrated by a pair of Palladian windows dressed nine different ways. For a clean, sophisticated look, Silhouette window shadings, right, have an understated elegance. Other options, from top, left to right: A refreshing splash of color from Duette honeycomb shades invigorates a neutral country room. In a modern, monochromatic setting, Lightlines miniblinds in a matte silver finish create a sleek backdrop for sculptural furnishings. Top-down pleated shades paired with gold damask curtains introduce rich color and texture into a Victorian-style parlor. For a retro-style scheme, white vertical blinds establish a clean, crisp background. The tailored lines of Vignette window shadings are well suited to the linear styling of Mission furniture. Simple window shades, updated with an easy clutch operation, create a surprisingly sharp look in a room where eclectic furnishings are the attention-getters. The rich grain of Country Woods blinds accented with coordinating cloth tape echoes the sumptuous texture of a kilim-covered chair and seagrass rug in a gentleman's study. For a refined sitting room, Luminette Privacy Sheers filter light and protect precious antiques.

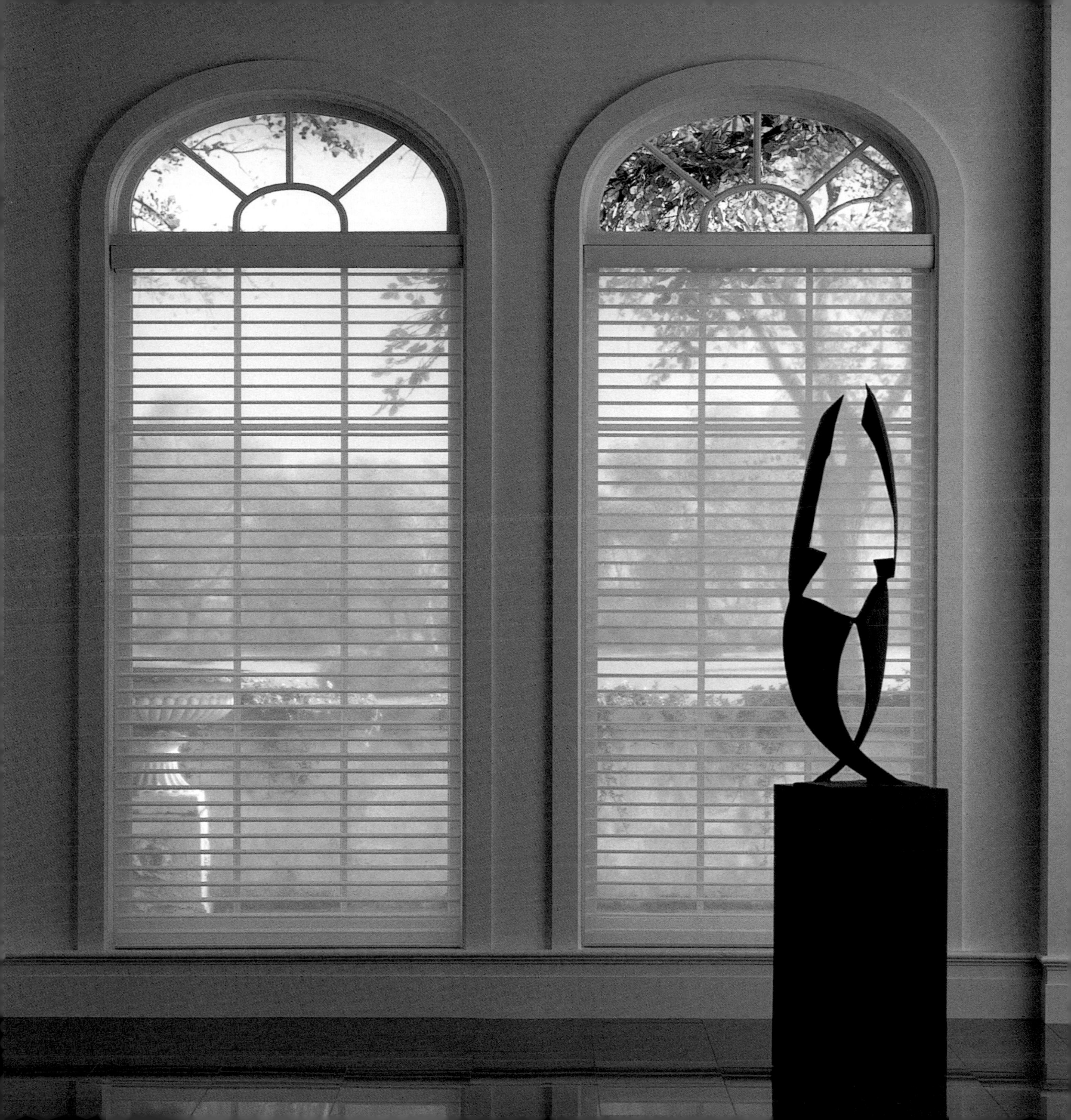

A wall of glass in a beach-house sitting room that overlooks the water was an ideal candidate for Duette Vertiglide shades. Vertiglide is essentially a honeycomb shade turned sideways—ideal for covering sliding glass doors or floor-to-ceiling windows. The semi-sheer antique-white fabric with 3/4-inch pleats admits light while cutting glare and providing a minimum of privacy. Fully open, Vertiglide stacks to a mere six inches wide.

The unique curved-track Duette Smart Shade hardware system, which can be motorized, allows any curved window to be covered. A conservatory in a townhouse, left, relaxes under an arched greenhouse ceiling covered with Duette honeycomb shades on Smart Shade mountings. A simple remote control opens the room fully or partially to dramatic views of the sky. Striking floor-to-ceiling windows in a slate-tiled bath by the sea, right, are fitted with Silhouette window shadings to let in sunlight and stunning views while still providing complete privacy when desired.

Beyond Woods hard-
wood blinds were
selected for light con-
trol in this sophisticated
gallery. The elegant texture
offers a subtle contrast to
the sleek furnishings.

THE GUIDE

Window fashions and treatments are decorating tools for solving the problems and making the most of the opportunities that exist at every window. Everything you need to know in order to choose appropriate and attractive coverings for your own windows is summed up in this section. The Guide answers your questions, identifies your practical needs, and shows how to bring comfort, style, and personality to windows of every shape, size, and location.

In an **1881 Victorian interior** designed by Louis Comfort Tiffany, an elegant layered look was achieved with print draperies, sheer curtains, a privacy shade, and a glass transom.

CLASSIC WINDOW TREATMENT STYLES

Spanish Colonial (1492–1850) freestanding shutters with handwrought screens combined the practical need to control light and heat with the beauty of Moorish design.

The **Renaissance** (ca. 1400–1600) saw a resurgence in the use of classical Greek and Roman forms at the window, notably in columns, pilasters, and cornices enhanced by rich fabrics in vivid colors. During the **French Renaissance** (1589–1643), windows were highlighted by heavy velvet or brocade draperies trimmed lavishly in gold braid. England's **Late Medieval Renaissance** (1558–1649)

featured Gothic windows with heavily leaded glass in diamond patterns. Curtains were strung by means of metal rings on metal or wood rods close to the glass, with solid wood shutters to help keep out wintry air.

The reign of the "Sun King," France's Louis XIV, during the **Baroque** period (1643–1730) was marked by much ornamentation and elaborate furnishings. Vivid hues, opulent fabrics, and rich textures characterized treatments for windows. Draperies were tied back low and given heavy fringe and elaborate top treatments. In the **English Baroque** or **Early Georgian** period (1660–1714), heavy cornices at the ceiling and draperies puddled on the floor denoted wealth and extravagance.

American Early Georgian (1700–1750), a scaled-down version of English Baroque, saw windows covered with raised-panel shutters, both for privacy and for insulation, as well as minimal swag-and-jabot overtreatments.

In the **Late Georgian** period (1751–1790), the rich reds, golds, and blues of the Chinese Chippendale style, in both imported and domestic fabrics, became the vogue. Draperies were fringed and tied back with tassels, and wood-slat venetian blinds gained popularity.

Previous page, elegant Duette honeycomb shades update pleated shades with energy-efficient construction. Right, time-honored elements—full-skirted drapes, a patterned ruffled valance—suit this room's historical character; the airiness of the treatment, however, is a modern touch.

The **Federal** period (1790–1820) introduced silk brocade, taffeta, satin, and voile to home interiors, hung asymmetrically and topped with swags. Upholstered, narrow cornices and double-tieback treatments were common.

The **Victorian Age** (1837–1901), along with the Industrial Revolution, produced a new class of nouveau riche, globe-trotting Americans, who brought back architectural ornaments and antiquities from their travels abroad to the Orient, Egypt, and Europe. These multiple influences were expressed in a cluttered, eclectic style reflected in ostentatious window

fashions. Interiors were darkened by an abundance of generous swags, layers of lace, and voluptuous overdraperies.

The **Arts and Crafts** movement, from the 1890s to about 1915 in the United States, reacted to the excesses of the Victorians with simple curtains in rough-woven fabrics or handblocked prints in an earth-toned palette. Handwork was emphasized through embroidered details on plain fabric panels and in stained-glass windows that eliminated the need for curtains.

The **Modern** movement in the early decades of this century embraced the leaner "form follows function" ideology of the German

Bauhaus and International movements. Curtaining and shading were downplayed as light itself became the primary element in defining windows.

In the 1930s, **Art Deco** marked a return to glamour and elegance in the home. Full, tailored overdraperies had high tiebacks and sleek decorative rods and other hardware that reflected the interests of the times, such as Egyptian motifs.

In the **postwar era,** the color spectrum of window fashions evolved from drab to dusty to brilliant. Scandinavian design inspired the use of printed fabrics in long and short draperies. The plate-glass

Playful pillows establish a retro look for a window-lined nook. The window treatments play along, matching a swagged valance in a rich fabric with practical Hunter Douglas Country Woods blinds with boldly contrasting tapes.

window was introduced as a popular form, and the first spring-tempered aluminum blind came on the market, as did vertical blinds.

Following the psychedelic excesses of **the 1960s,** a revival of traditional colors and styles was observed as authentic early American window treatments were devised for newly restored homes. At the same time, a contemporary, clean look became popular as sleek miniblinds moved from the workplace to the home. A few years later, opulent English country chintz was one of the most popular window fashion statements of **the 1980s.**

During **the 1990s,** expressive personal style, typically more casual than formal, has superseded specific trends, with mix-and-match borrowings of period and regional influ-

ences gaining favor. A new generation of window fashions that both welcome and control light and views has more than met the challenges of design without the dictates of strict rules.

The antithesis of Victorian ornamentation, above, is found in the streamlined look of Luminette Privacy Sheers, below, which combine the best qualities of sheers and blinds.

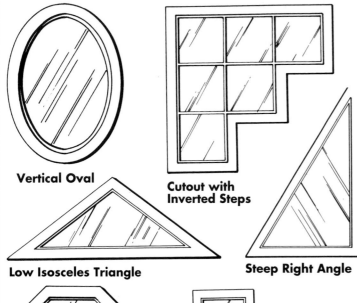

Vertical Oval

Cutout with Inverted Steps

Low Isosceles Triangle

Steep Right Angle

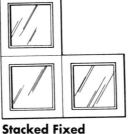

Octagon

Stacked Fixed

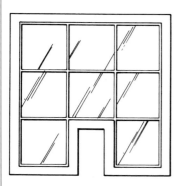

Cutout

Cathedral

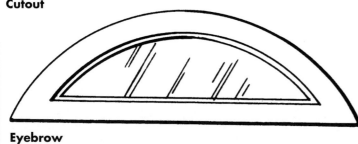

Eyebrow

WINDOW STYLES

A glossary of common and specialty window styles.

A-Frame – a large window with an angled top that follows the line of a slanted roof or ceiling.

Bay – three or more windows set at angles to each other within a recessed area.

Bow – a curved window that forms an arc extending outward from the wall.

Casement – a crank-operated window that opens either inward or outward.

Clerestory – a shallow window set near the ceiling.

Corner – two windows that meet in a corner.

Dormer – a small window projecting from the house in an alcove-like extension.

Double – two windows set side by side, usually double-hung.

Double-Hung – a two-sash window in which one or both sashes slide up and down.

Eyebrow – a half oval or ellipse, often installed as a dormer.

French/Atrium Doors – a pair of doors with glass panes; with French doors, both sides open; only one door opens with atrium style.

Gothic Arch – an arch whose curves meet in a point at the top.

For hard-to-reach rectangular windows, such as this pair of skylights, the Duette shade with Simplicity hardware is the answer to controlling light from above. The shade opens and closes with the aid of a handle and skylight wand.

Greenhouse – curved vertical windows that form both the walls and the ceiling of a sunroom.

Jalousie – narrow, horizontal slats of glass maneuvered by a crank.

Octagon – a modified circle formed of eight sides of equal length; a hexagon has six sides.

Palladian/Arch – a classical window form distinguished by its graceful arch.

Picture – a wide window designed to frame a view; usually a fixed center glass pane with side windows that open.

Ranch – a wide, high-off-the-floor window with sliding sashes.

Skylight – a window inserted into the roof or ceiling.

Sliding Glass Door – a modern version of the French door with two or three large panes, at least one of which slides to open.

ENERGY EFFICIENCY AND ROOM COMFORT

Many window styles call for energy conservation measures to reduce heating and air-conditioning costs and to assure that a room is as comfortable as possible. Blinds and shades, on their own or in combination with curtains and draperies, can be selected for their special ability to insulate from the effects of heat and cold. Honeycomb shades, reflective metal finishes available on pleated fabric shades, and

A custom dormer window playfully echoes the architecture of the house while helping illuminate a dark alcove.

A round window with a ship's wheel pattern adds interest to a peaked roof facade and light to an attic.

blackout linings are three of the many options that help reduce energy loss.

To ensure energy efficiency, look for window treatments with a high R-value, which is a measure of the material's resistance to heat loss. A single layer of glass has an R-value of .88, while double-glazed windows generally measure 1.75.

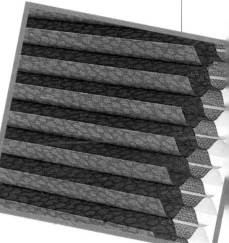

Duette triple-cell honeycomb shades, shown here in a print that creates a dappled light pattern, are highly energy-efficient.

In a room where Palladian windows are the focal point but the view is not, Duette honeycomb shades with a Duolite hardware system screen the view and make the best of the light. Two different shades—one sheer, the other blackout—operate from the same moving center rail with individual controls to allow adjustment for privacy and light.

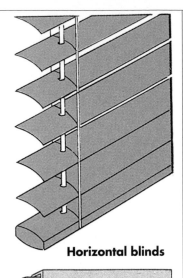

Horizontal blinds

Vertical blinds

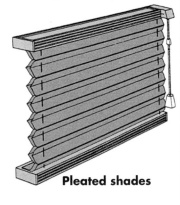

Pleated shades

Window treatments can increase the R-value dramatically. Honeycomb shades are generally the most energy-efficient because their cellular construction traps air and acts as an insulator; double and triple honeycombs have additional layers of air pockets for even greater heat retention. The Hunter Douglas triple-cell honeycomb shade, with an R-value of 4.8, is considered the most energy-efficient shade on the market. Vertical blinds offer the next best level of insulation, and pleated shades also rate well, with an R-value of about 2.5.

Window treatments can also help reduce heat gain in summer. The Summer Shading Coefficient is a measure of this ability; in this case, the lower the number, the better. Honeycomb shades excel at reducing heat gain, as well as providing good sound absorption.

A final consideration is ultraviolet protection. The UV rays in sunlight can cause natural undyed fabrics to yellow and upholstery and drapery fabrics, furnishings, artwork, and even wood floors to fade. Depending on the opacity of the fabric chosen, window shadings, pleated shades, and honeycomb shades all provide good (90 to 99 percent) UV blockage.

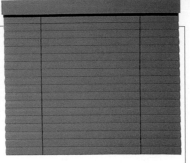

CREATING WINDOW FASHIONS WITH BLINDS AND SHADES

The classic looks and down-to-earth practicality of blinds and shades make them ideal choices for bringing a sense of style to both modern and traditional interiors. In design language, a blind is a tailored window covering

Traditional blinds, left, allow light through cord holes. The Hunter Douglas de-Light feature, above, eliminates this problem by offsetting holes to the backs of the slats.

consisting of horizontal slats or vertical vanes, which can be opened and closed, made from sturdy materials such as aluminum, vinyl, or wood. A shade is a window covering

made from soft fabric or fabric-like material, thus lending itself to a broad range of decorative styles. It most commonly rolls or folds up from bottom to top.

Both the streamlined design of blinds and the visual softness of shades offer beauty and function in a neat package; each is capable of standing on its own or combining with lavish layers of draperies and top treatments for a highly personalized window statement.

Horizontal blinds are the contemporary version of the venetian blinds that date back to the 17th century. The blind con-

sists of slats that can be stacked up by means of a pull cord. Another control tilts the slats for as much light control and privacy as desired.

Versatile horizontal blinds can be used alone, with top treatments, or as undertreatments in combination with draperies, and can be manufactured to fit almost any

size and shape of window. They are available with aluminum, wood, vinyl, or fabric slats.

Aluminum blinds come with slats ranging from micro (1/2") to mini (1") to broader (2") widths. Their clean-lined design makes them suitable in almost any room decor. They are particularly compatible with modern architecture. Miniblinds can be cut to fit around air conditioners and window cranks, and custom-fitted to unusual window shapes. Stacking space for aluminum blinds is minimal; a 6' blind

Hunter Douglas Country Woods blinds, left, screen light and views and lend traditional cachet to a study. Aluminum blinds, above, come in finishes from metallics to suede.

SAFETY FEATURES FOR SHADES AND BLINDS

Hunter Douglas is committed to protecting the safety of children and pets through a range of patented devices. The Break-Thru safety tassel comes standard on all horizontal aluminum and wood blinds. This two-part plastic tassel snaps together to contain window cords neatly, but breaks apart under minimal pressure should a child or pet get tangled in the cord. The Break-Thru tassel is also sold over-the-counter to retrofit any make or model of horizontal blinds. On vertical blinds, the PermAssure safety wand replaces the control cord and chain with an easy-to-use wand that opens and rotates the blind. And on shades with cord loops, such as Silhouette window shadings and Duette Easy Rise honeycomb shades, a cord tensioner pulley, permanently mounted to the sill or frame, keeps the cord taut at all times. Cord cleats are also available for neatly and safely containing loose cords. The PowerRise remote control option does away with shade cords altogether and allows you to raise and lower them at the touch of a button; the safety stop feature halts movement as soon as the shade touches any obstruction.

The Break-Thru safety tassel opens easily under pressure, above, in case children get entangled in the cord, but snaps back together neatly.

The PowerRise safety stop prevents shades from closing if anything is in the way, top. The PermAssure safety wand eliminates worries about kids getting tangled in vertical blind cords, left.

stacks to less than 6" fully raised.

Hunter Douglas offers dozens of enamel finishes, textures, and colors, including suede textures, faux finishes, and metallics. The new matte SoftSuede finish offers a warmer, richer look than previously available in aluminum blinds. And the unique Dust Shield paint-coating system reduces static electricity and inhibits dust build-up on blinds to reduce maintenance. Duotone blinds combine a decorator color on one side of the slats with a neutral color on the other so that the closed blinds present a uniform exterior appearance. And the new de-Light feature on sophisticated Lightlines blinds eliminates the problem of light leakage by positioning slats closer together and concealing cord holes at the backs of the slats.

Wood blinds, valued for their handsome, natural look, durability, and insulating properties, come in 1", 2", and 3" slat widths. More expensive than aluminum blinds, the best wood blinds are made of natural American hardwoods such as ash, cherry, oak, basswood, or maple as well as pine, and are kiln-dried to prevent warping, splitting, or twisting. Finishes on

Hunter Douglas Country Woods blinds include traditional wood stains as well as washed and painted looks; in addition, premium Artisan Series wood blinds can be custom-colored to match any fabric, wallpaper, or paint. For added decorative impact, the woven cloth tapes on wood blinds may be chosen in coordinating or contrasting colors. For maximum light control, the de-Light feature, available on all Hunter Douglas wood blinds, blocks light penetration.

Wrapped wood, a new option from Hunter Douglas Beyond Woods hardwood blinds, brings elegance and variety to hardwood blinds by adding decorative surface finishes such as bird's-eye maple, burled

mahogany, stippled glazes, and whitewashed and weathered looks.

Faux wood blinds, also new, are an economical alternative to natural wood blinds. In high-moisture locations or humid climates, they offer the rich look of wood with unparalleled dimensional stability and durability.

Vertical blinds, first introduced in 1948, are now available in a full range of finishes and textures, from moderately priced vinyl and aluminum to top-of-the-line fabrics. With vanes that traverse and rotate smoothly, they offer the ultimate in privacy and light control.

The vertical line of these blinds complements most window shapes and adds height to a

Decorative finishes from bird's-eye maple to a whitewashed look lend distinction to Hunter Douglas Beyond Woods hardwood blinds.

The sleek profile of Lightlines spring-tempered aluminum blinds is achieved by a curved headrail. It functions as a built-in valance to conceal brackets and to project an all-in-one appearance at the window.

Chosen to harmonize with the muted wall color, right, Hunter Douglas Country Woods blinds efficiently control light in a sun-filled room.

room. Used alone, with coordinating hard valances or fabric top treatments, or as drapery undertreatments, they suit most decorating styles beautifully. The Vertical Specialty System from Hunter Douglas permits verticals to be used in bow, bay, angled, arched, and Palladian window installations as well as skylights. And the Masquerade custom valance system offers coordinating tiered valances to enhance the style of the blinds

The new Paramount Contoured Headrail from Hunter Douglas creates a sleek look for vertical blinds.

while concealing traditional track system hardware.

The Paramount Contoured Headrail from Hunter Douglas provides an even sleeker, more integrated look for vertical blinds, creating a flawless, finished appearance from top to bottom.

Verticals "stack," or compress, tightly when opened, taking up much less space than draperies. When closed, the vanes overlap closely, keeping out heat in summer and cold in winter. The vertical position of the vanes prevents dust from collecting—gravity does the job of dusting for you.

Vinyl verticals are made from sturdy PVC that will not twist or bow with age. Vinyl vanes come in both neutral and vivid colors and a variety of textures and finishes. There are even sculptured vinyl louvers that create distinctive shapes and patterns, ideal for contemporary interiors.

Aluminum vanes have baked enamel finishes for long-lasting brightness, plus the added benefits of easy maintenance and moderate prices.

Fabric verticals add a touch of warmth and softness to the window treatment. Free-hanging fabric vanes are weighted to maintain straightness. Fabric insert verticals use strips of the fabric of your choice inserted into solid vinyl backings with clear grooved edges. Inserts also allow you to display a neutral color scheme on the outward side seen through the window and a different decorator color on the room side.

Pleated fabric shades first came to this country from the Netherlands in the 1970s and are now one of the most popular window fashions, lending their crisp, stylish look to any window

The crinkled cotton of sophisticated, contemporary pleated shades softly diffuses light and adds textural interest.

as a solitary treatment or in combination with draperies. A 6' fabric shade stacks to under 3", making this an ideal undertreatment for draperies that virtually disappears when raised. The permanent pleats come in 1" widths. The shade's separate backing layer offers high energy efficiency, complete control of light and privacy, and a uniform exterior appearance with a choice of room-side colors.

Metallized pleated shades are available in transparent, sheer fabrics that allow light in or semiprivate fabrics that softly diffuse light by day and add privacy by night. They are very energy-efficient, reducing heat loss in winter by as much as 50 percent and heat gain in

summer as much as 80 percent. Also, bonded aluminum backing on metallized pleated shades filters the sun's rays and helps prevent fading of carpets and furniture. Two fabrics can be combined in one shade, one installed above and the other below a traveling center rail, allowing you to choose a sheer for day or an opaque fabric at night with the pull of a cord.

Nonmetallized pleated shades come in a choice of interesting fabrics including lace and eyelet, and in textures that evoke silk, linen, and even satin. Many are

Vanes on Hunter Douglas fabric verticals are available in more colors than ever before, making it easy to complement any decor.

REMOTE-CONTROL SHADES

The PowerRise remote control system, available with Duette honeycomb shades, Silhouette window shadings, and additional products, raises and lowers shades at the touch of a button: Just point the sleek remote at the infrared eye on the headrail.

The remote is battery-operated and requires no wiring, so installation is both simple and affordable. Thanks to a convenient memory stop feature, shades can be automatically opened to the same level every day, and a safety stop is instantly activated when the shade touches an object in its path. If decorative top treatments cover the headrail, an optional satellite eye can be positioned adjacent to it.

PowerRise offers point-and-click convenience for raising and lowering honeycomb shades and other Hunter Douglas products.

available with matching cut yardage fabric to create coordinated accessories.

The versatile pleated shade is equally at home on standard and special-shape windows, as well as in various unique applications. One solution for sliding glass doors or extra-wide windows is to hang multiple shades from a single headrail; each shade can then be raised or lowered independently.

Manhattan shades maintain the shape of their 1/2" pleats permanently, thanks to exclusive TruePleat construction.

Hunter Douglas Duette honeycomb shades come in single-, double-, and triple-cell configurations, and in 3/8", 1/2", 3/4", and 2" pleat sizes.

Cellular shades, introduced in 1985, are made in a unique pleated construction resembling the honeycomb of a beehive, an important energy-saving feature. Duette honeycomb shades are available with single, double, or triple cells. They can be used either horizontally in 3/8", 1/2", 3/4", or 2" pleat sizes, or vertically in 3/4" or 2" pleat sizes. The shade fabrics are available in four degrees of transparency for privacy and light control, from sheer to semi-opaque (the original Duette fabric) to blackout. Duette Duolite offers a dual-fabric option, combining a semi-sheer on top and an opaque fabric on the bottom, for example, for the ultimate in flexible light control.

Fabrics come in a wide spectrum of colors and patterns, including prints, textures, and faux marble and granite finishes. The premier

Manhattan shade has 1/2" pleats with exclusive TruePleat construction so that the pleats keep their shape permanently. Manhattan shades boast a range of designer fabrics, including the look of raw silk, linen, pinpoint, and rattan textures. Sleek, low-profile headrails, bottom rails, and color-coordinated hardware assure that the shades blend in beautifully with the most elegant window treatments.

The tailored look of this window covering complements most window styles, from simple casements to challenging bows. Cellular shades are often considered a contemporary alternative to sheers: They can be used alone, with a simple top treatment, or under full draperies. The softness of the fabric combined

with crisp pleating yields a look equally at home in traditional or modern interiors.

Specialty tracking systems enable Ductte shades to fit the tight radius of bay or greenhouse window curves as well as skylights. Duette arches are also available.

Raising or lowering large shades is simplified by a clutch-and-pulley headrail system, operated manually or motorized. An adaptable hardware system such as Vertiglide allows Duette honeycomb shades to be mounted vertically and open to one side for sliding glass or French doors

or room dividers. No matter how large the shades, they stack to just 6".

Luminette **Privacy Sheers,** the newest innovation from Hunter Douglas, achieve the seemingly impossible, melding the light-softening quality of sheer draperies with the privacy and adjustable control of blinds. Vertical vanes of soft fabric are bonded to a single sheer facing fabric. When the sheers are drawn closed, the vanes can be rotated with the twist of a wand to provide priva-

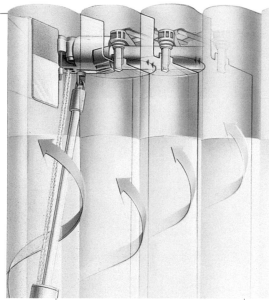

Light floods a cozy living area through Luminette Privacy Sheers, which form a striking backdrop with their height and long, elegant lines.

The sheer casing of Luminette contains vanes that rotate closed for light control, above. This versatility makes it ideal for such settings as bathrooms, below, where a fine balance between privacy and the desire for light is needed.

Silhouette window shadings offer light-filtering qualities plus the functionality of blinds.

cy, or tilted open for filtered light. Luminette reduces glare and provides UV protection during the day, while providing a soft-focus view; by night, it offers complete privacy with the luxurious look of draperies. When an unobstructed view is desired, the sheers stack neatly to one side or open at the center to stack on both sides of a window or glazed door. Luminette is available in a range of quiet neutrals in either a classic sheer or a softly textured fabric that accents its vertical lines. An integral fabric heading unobtrusively conceals the operating mechanism.

Luminette sheers are a natural choice for French doors, sliding doors and walls of windows, where both light and privacy are a priority. They are equally at home in traditional antique-filled interiors and in spare contemporary spaces.

Silhouette **window shadings** are another remarkable new category of window coverings offering the best of all possible worlds: the light control of a blind, the easy operation of a shade, and the soft, light-filtering translucence of a sheer curtain. The shade is composed of soft fabric vanes suspended between two panels of sheer knit facing. When the shade is lowered, the fabric slats can be tilted open for a softly diffused view or closed to allow varying degrees of privacy. When raised, the shade is completely concealed within a color-coordinated headrail, which can be mounted inside or outside the window frame.

Four fabric choices—woven, linen, crinkle-textured, and a room-darkening semi-opaque material—add the subtle dimension of texture with varying levels of opacity. The vanes are available in 2" or bold 3" widths. Nantucket window shadings offer a special collection of casual fabrics in a 2 1/2" vane size.

Light and soft-focus views are admitted when the fabric vanes of Silhouette window shadings are opened.

In a traditional room, a textured fabric gives cascading Vignette window shadings an understated richness.

Silhouette window shadings can be operated by a single control cord, by a hardwired motorized switch, or by the PowerRise battery operated remote control system. In addition, arch and angled windows can be fitted with shadings with nonadjustable, open vanes.

Silhouette makes a striking design statement on its own; it also blends easily into any decor, and may be combined with a top treatment or traditional draperies.

ished look on their own, or they can be used in conjunction with simple top treatments or draperies. They work especially well on windows where the beauty of the light-filtering fabric can be appreciated.

Roller shades are the most basic of window treatments, functional yet still fashionable. Typically made of vinyl, they can also be crafted from fabric, wooden or bamboo slats, mesh screening, or even dyed film. Hunter Douglas has replaced the standard spring-loaded roller with a clutch system and continuous cord and pulley that allow for easier, more controlled positioning of the shade—and eliminate the snap-backs typical of conventional shades.

A choice of fabrics and decorative hem styles with a variety of trims, plus wood and vinyl valances, add a decorator touch to roller shades. They can also be configured with a

reverse roll so that the roller is concealed by the fabric. Roller shades can be installed on single, double-hung or casement style windows and are most often used as a practical undertreatment beneath draperies or valances.

Fabric shades, offering the elegance and romance of custom soft shades, originated in Europe, with some of today's most popular styles dating back to the 1800s. The three most versatile fabric shades are balloon, Roman, and Austrian.

With fabrics in a broad range of colors and textures, Vignette window shadings adapt easily to both casual and formal settings.

Vignette window shadings have the gentle draping and tailored appearance of Roman shades with the easy, controlled operation of a cord-operated shade. The softly folded front fabric is joined to a knit rear fabric for a consistently smooth, crisp appearance. Available in a choice of 3" or 4" fold sizes, Vignette comes in a wide range of fabrics and colors, from a satin weave to a nubby linen texture to striped seersuckers that seem to glow in sunlight, from jewel tones such as purple and cranberry to tone-on-tone stripes in emerald and royal blue, from white jacquard to gauzy ribbon fabric in pale

shades. The fabric is anti-static as well as dust- and stain-resistant. And unlike traditional Roman shades, Vignette will not flatten, wrinkle, or sag. A solid white knit fabric backing provides a unified look from the exterior.

Vignette window shadings, which can be mounted inside or outside the window frame, have a fin-

Colorful tone-on-tone stripes such as these from Carole Fabrics, above, are versatile decorating choices. Below, Silhouette window shadings provide the luminous undertreatment for a large window adorned with valance, draperies, and shade in striped fabric.

Balloon shades, above, combine the privacy of blinds when lowered with the beauty and fullness of draperies when raised.

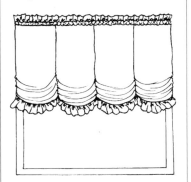

Balloon shade

Balloon shades, combining the privacy of blinds with the beauty and fullness of draperies, are cherished for the distinctive billows that form as the shade is raised. The box-pleated balloon shade has a more tailored appearance, while the softer shirred shade is more feminine.

Balloon shades can be made of soft, drapable fabrics as well as crisp, lightweight ones. They can be used on their own as operating shades, in lieu of sheers with tied-back draperies for a rich, layered look, or as stationary valances.

Roman shades are simple, flat fabric shades that draw up in neat, even folds rather than in poufs, giving them a tailored look suitable in all decors—traditional, contemporary, transition-

98

al, or country. A softer version has horizontal folds across the full width of the shade to create texture and dimension even when the shade is fully lowered. Both styles can be fabricated as operating shades or as stationary valances. They look best in crisp, medium-weight fabrics.

Austrian shades are found in formal, elegant settings because of their rich appearance. This style of soft shade is generally made with 2-to-1 fullness across the width and 3-to-1 fullness in length. The extra volume creates a scalloped bottom and elegant ruching across the face of the shade. Sheer fabrics are the most popular choice for Austrian shades, but they can also be striking in cotton prints and other medium-weight fabrics, especially when used as valances.

Shutters, highly popular for centuries and still valued for their practicality and traditional looks, may be made of solid wood but most often have movable slats to admit light and views. A more recent innovation is shutters made of PolySatin

vinyl. These have the advantage of being warp- and crack-proof, which suits them to high-usage and high-humidity locations such as bathrooms and kitchens, as well as other areas. Hunter Douglas offers two styles in its Palm Beach line: Lantana, which can be opened and shut with a flick of the fingers, and Palmetto, operated by a classic pull-bar. Both come in 2 1/4" and 3 1/4" blade sizes in one of two off-whites, and will not fade or peel.

A delicate Austrian shade adds a romantic dimension to a bathroom overlooking a secluded garden, above, offering some privacy without obscuring the window's pleasing architectural lines.

Made of a PolySatin compound that won't warp, chip, or fade, Hunter Douglas Lantana shutters incorporate a gear system that opens or closes all the louvers simultaneously with a flick of the fingers.

Shutters

DRAPERY ABCs

The terms "draperies" and "curtains" are often used interchangeably, but each has different characteristics. "Drapery" describes a pleated fabric usually meant to be drawn open or closed by means of a pull cord, while "curtain" refers to fabric that is shirred or gathered onto a rod. Both draperies and curtains require a range of hardware, encompassing everything from rods to decorative tiebacks, holdbacks, and swagholders, for hanging and creating a customized appearance.

Traverse rod – the conventional hardware along which draperies move with the pull of a cord. When draperies are closed, rod is hidden; when opened, rod is visible unless concealed by a top treatment. Drapes can either draw one way or split-draw from the center.

Decorative traverse rod – an inexpensive alternative to top treatments; rod, rings, brackets, and end finials are mounted to be visible above the drapery heading.

Hand traverse rod – available in a variety of styles and sizes, including wood poles and metal café rods. Drapery hangs below rod from rings and is opened by hand.

A combination of hard and soft treatments—classic shutters with wide slats and draperies caught back to reveal the textured lining fabric—create an interesting tableau at a window.

Shirred drapery rod – an acrylic or metal rod or wood pole that is threaded through a "casing" or "rod pocket" in the drapery heading to create a gathered or shirred look.

Tieback – a piece of fabric cut in any of several styles (straight, contoured, braided, gathered, etc.) that is used to hold a drapery panel back; draperies look best when tied back about a third of the distance from the top or the bottom of the treatment.

Holdback – a piece of decorative hardware that performs the same function as a tieback.

Swagholder – special hardware that allows fabric to be swagged in innumerable ways by pulling it through an open loop.

CUSTOMIZED TOPPERS

The area above the window treatment can be the room's crowning glory, depending on how you choose to top it.

Heading – the top portion of a window treatment; various looks can be achieved by tabbing, pleating, or shirring.

Top treatment – any of a wide range of fabric treatments, primarily decorative, that literally crown a window arrangement. It can be used alone, over a blind or shade, or as the finishing touch to custom draperies.

Valance – a top treatment constructed from fabric; it may be flat,

Passementerie like this colorful cording and the trimmings at right, from Carole Fabrics, add a decorator flourish to fabric treatments.

pleated, or gathered, and may hang from a board or a rod.

Cornice – a top treatment constructed on a wood frame, padded and covered with fabric. Cornices can also be made entirely from wood or other materials

and given special profiles and finishes, such as the collection of architectural cornices, valances, and moldings from Hunter Douglas.

Swag – a top treatment with fabric that falls gracefully from the top of a board or a pole, looping downward and then back to the top; several swags can be overlapped on wide windows and combined with cascades or jabots for decorative effect.

Trimming – any of a broad range of rich embellishments for top treatments, also known as passementerie. These include fringe, tassels, braid, cording, and gimp.

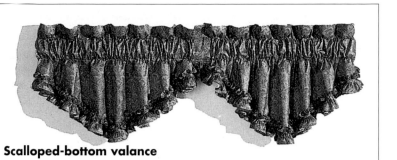

Scalloped-bottom valance

Passementerie   **Cornices**

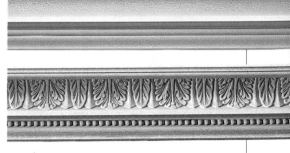

Shirred-on-the-rod valance

Decorative traverse rod

Conventional traverse rod

Standard decorative holdback

A fully decorated girl's bedroom window combines an Austrian shade, shirred-on-the rod curtains, coordinating tiebacks, and a matching ruffled valance.

PLANNING WINDOW TREATMENTS

ELEMENTS OF DESIGN

Space defines the boundaries and sets the limits on the area to be decorated. The space most directly affecting window treatments is the area immediately surrounding the window, including the wall and the window itself.

Key Questions:

● Is there enough wall space to extend the treatment comfortably beyond the window?

● Is there so much space above the window that your treatment should encompass that space?

● Is the space so limiting that the treatment must be installed on or very close to the frame?

Space-Altering Solutions:

● A room that appears small looks best with a simple window treatment that blends with the walls and creates the perception of greater space.

● In an oversize space, a multilayered treatment helps give the impression of a cozier, warmer room.

Line, straight or curved, is the beginning point of all design. Straight lines include horizontals, diagonals, and verticals. The mood of a room can be altered by observing some guidelines:

● Horizontal lines create a sense of breadth, width, and size.

● Vertical lines add height, dignity, and formality.

● Diagonal lines attract attention and lead the eye, but they need to be supported by verticals or opposing diagonals so as not to be disturbing.

● Curved lines are romantic and feminine. They are used to soften or relieve straight lines in a room.

Form is the result of lines joining to produce an overall shape. You can alter or emphasize the shape of a window by the treatment you select.

Windows come in all shapes and sizes, but most finished window treatments are rectangles. The straight lines of a rectangle can be softened with a gathered heading or the gentle folds of a swag and jabots. Conversely, the rectangular form can be emphasized with vertical banding or stationary side panels of fabric.

Window-Altering Solutions:

● Full side-panel draperies combined with a beyond-the-frame cornice can make a narrow window seem wider.

● A short window can be made to appear taller with the addition of an above-the-frame valance in combination with floor-length sheers and tied-back side panels.

Texture refers to the surface quality, whether rough or smooth. Smooth, shiny surfaces are more formal; rough, coarse surfaces more casual. The use of a combination of textures in a room adds variety, but

one should dominate. A room decorated primarily in slick, shiny textures needs rougher textures for contrast and variation.

Choosing Textured Fabrics:

● Texture alters the color of fabric. A nubby fabric has shadows, which makes the fabric look darker. Shiny fabrics reflect light and appear lighter to the eye.

● Shiny fabrics, because they are reflective, also recede; coarse fabrics absorb light and appear to take up additional space in the room.

● While a combination of textures adds interest to window treatments, sharp contrast in texture should be used only for dramatic effect.

One effective use of color at the window features Country Woods chosen in a finish to contrast with the background color of the wall and with cloth tapes that coordinate with the upholstery.

● Window treatments of nubby, coarse fabrics look best at 2-to-1 fullness. The reduced fullness accommodates the bulk of the fabric and minimizes the visual weight of the finished treatment.

PROPORTION AND SCALE

A window treatment pleasing to the eye obeys classic principles of proportion and scale:

● The placement of tiebacks affects the visual weight of a window. The correct placement is a third of the distance from either top or bottom.

● Use top treatments that are approximately one-fifth of the total treatment length.

● If cascades are not floor-length, they should fall even with another design feature such as a windowsill, chair rail, or muntin.

● Avoid hanging draperies with no visual reference point. Whenever possible, line up their hems with a windowsill, apron, or floor.

● In determining the scale of window treatments, their actual size as well as their visual weight should be compatible with other furnishings in the room.

COLOR

The most important single element in decorating a room, including its windows, is the effective use of color.

When selecting colors for window fashions, keep in mind:

● The unchangeable elements in the room, as dictated by budget, aesthetics, and structural limitations.

● The size of the room.

● The location and exposure of the room.

● The amount of natural light.

● The room's function.

● Who will use the room.

● The decorating style desired.

The visual effects of color used in a window treatment will vary according to many factors:

● A brightly colored window treatment against a light background advances and fills the space. The same treatment against a dark background will not look as large or bright.

● A brightly colored treatment against walls of a lighter value of the same color will appear to blend in with the walls.

● To draw attention to a window treatment, use a bright color against a lighter value of its complement. To minimize the treatment, surround it with colors of the same value.

● Medium-value prints against a white background are easy to see at a distance; in neutrals, the same pattern is less eye-catching.

● The surface of a fabric affects its color intensity. A slick, shiny fabric such as satin or chintz will look more intensely red than the identical red on homespun linen.

● Subtle color contrasts make a room feel formal, calm, feminine. Bold color contrasts make a room feel informal, cozy, masculine.

● Color affects the appearance of lines. Horizontal lines in any color widen a window treatment; vertical colored lines against a contrasting ground add height.

● Warm colors visually advance, cool colors recede.

A prominent window is integrated into the color scheme of a family room with Duette honeycomb shades.

● Balance colors throughout the room. One hue should cover as much as two-thirds of an area, with a second color covering nearly a third. Other colors act as accents. Repeating colors around a room or using a progression of values of a single color—light green for the walls, darker greens for draperies, furniture, and carpet—creates visual rhythm.

RESOURCES

A directory of Hunter Douglas window fashion products. For more information about any of these products, call 1-800-937-7895.

Horizontal Blinds

Lightlines® mini- and microblinds
Decor® mini- and microblinds
Celebrity® miniblinds
Country Woods® wood blinds
Country Woods® Classics
Country Woods® Select
Country Woods® Artisan Series
Beyond Woods™ hardwood blinds
Everwood™ faux wood blinds
Wood Mates™ faux wood blinds
Magnaflex™
SoftSuede™ finish
Dust Shield™
de-Light® feature

Vertical Blinds

Millenia™ custom vertical blinds
Passages vertical blinds
Hunter Douglas Vertical Specialty Systems
Complements PVC vertical blinds
Masquerade vertical valance system
Paramount™ track system

Pleated Shades

Cellular Shades

Duette® honeycomb shades
The Manhattan® Collection of Duette® honeycomb shades
The Originals Collection™
Chelsea™
Gramercy Park™
Soho™

Park Avenue™
Park Avenue Eclipse™
Tiffany Silk™
LinenSoft™
Tribeca™
TruePleat™
Applause® honeycomb shades
Applause® Affinity™
Applause® Legends™
Applause II® honeycomb shades

Privacy Sheers

Luminette Privacy Sheers®
Angelica™
Linea™
SofTrak™ system

Window Shades

Window Shadings

Nantucket™ window shadings
Silhouette® window shadings
Bon Soir™
Naturelle™
Originale™
Toujours™
Vignette® window shadings

Cornices, Valances, and Architectural Moldings

Hardware Systems

Duette® Duolite®
Duette® Easy Glide®
Duette® Easy Rise®
Duette® Simplicity®
Duette® Skyrise®
Duette® Smart Shade®
Duette® Vertiglide®
Manhattan® Easy Rise®
Manhattan® Simplicity®
Manhattan® Skyrise®
Permaclear™ vertical groover
Color Mates™ vertical groover
PERMALIGN™ track system
PermAssure™ wand control system

PermaTilt™ wand control system
PosiTilt™ carrier system
SofTrak™ system

Safety Products

Break-Thru® miniblind safety tassel
Hunter Douglas cord tensioner
PermAssure™ wand control system

ACKNOWLEDGMENTS

Special Consultants

Martin Lipsitt
Elizabeth Jane Pavelle

Copy Editor

Joal K. Hetherington

Contributing Photographers

Jean Mitchel Allsopp page 20 • **Jeremiah Bean** page 91 far right • **Laurie Black** page 26 • **Peter Brauné** pages 11, 13 top, 35, 36 top, 51, 69, 84, 85, 91 center, 92 top, 93 bottom, 94 top right, 97 bottom • **Jerry Cailor** pages 37 top, 43, 62 top and bottom • **Ron Crofoot** pages 2, 28-29, 36-37 bottom, 81 • **Craig Cutler** page 94 bottom center, 97 top right • **Decorage** pages 96-97 center • **Gary Denys** pages 52 left, 70 bottom • **Nicholas DeSciose** pages 54-55, 90-91 center, 92 bottom right • **David Glomb** page 68 • **John Hall** page 15 • **Jenifer Jordan** pages 98 top left and bottom, 101 bottom • **Michael Lupino** pages 4, 10, 21, 38, 46-47, 66 bottom, 87 bottom right, 95 bottom • © **Peter Maas/Esto** pages 12-13 bottom • **Minh + Wass** cover and pages 18-19, 50, 61, 63, 71 bottom, 78-79, 96 bottom • **Michael Peck** pages 16, 39, 64-65 • **Bill Rothschild** page 87 top • **Joseph Standart** pages 48,

92 bottom left • **William Stites** pages 34, 40-41, 44, 45, 53 right, 56, 57, 60, 67, 82-83, 96 top left, 102 top • **UPPA Limited, London** page 80 • **Visual Concepts, High Point, NC** pages 8-9, 23, 24-25, 30, 31, 49 bottom, 58-59, 66 top, 71 top, 72-73, 88, 89 bottom, 102-103 bottom • **Brian Vanden Brink** page 14 • **Dale Wing** page 17 • **Bruce Wolfe** pages 7, 22, 42, 52-53 bottom, 74, 76-77, 91 right, 99 bottom, 103 right

Interior Designers

Perry Bentley page 20 • **Sig Bergamin** page 15 • **Christopher Coleman** page 50 • **Sandra D'Amata** page 61 • **Thom Filicia** pages 18-19 • **Jamie Gibbs** pages 49 top, 86-87 center • **Ron Rezek** page 68 • **Jody Rose** page 26 • **Susan Thorn** pages 40-41, 56, 82-83 • **Nancy Wing** page 17

Stylists

Peter Frank • page 7 • **Audrey Lee** cover and pages 18-19,50, 61, 63, 78-79, 96 bottom • **Christopher Maia** page 48 **Nina Sheffly** pages 4, 10, 21, 22, 38, 43, 46-47

Color Consultant for Hunter Douglas

Barbara Schirmeister

Illustrations

David Euell page 95 top **Victoria and Albert Museum** pages 12 left, 86 top

We would like to thank the following companies:

New Glass page 60 • **Pella** pages 70, 89 top • **Palazzetti** page 60